Resume 101

Fine tuning a Resume and Cover Letter

Daniel A. Garcia

Dedication

This is dedicated to the educators, teaching business communication courses.

Thank you.

Go Get 'EM!

How To Use

This journal is made up of the following:

- Check list: To give a visual of what was worked on. Check off tips and questions.

- Note section: To make note of improvement.

Divided into three (3) sections:

- Resume structure.

- Cover Letter structure.

- Interview tips.

Resume Structure

For those first starting out – in writing up a resume; it can be a little hard and/or difficult to highlight who you are. When applying for a job – the committee needs to be able to see your highlights in your education, work experience, or whatever makes you qualified for the position.

This section, will assist you; when doing your resume.

The following section contains:
- Resume layout and example.
- Checklist/Critical questions: to check off as you go.
- Note section: to make additional notes.

➢ You can use a free template with Word. Convert the document, into a PDF – when sending in your resume.

Your Name

555 your address   (777)cell number

City, state, zip code   email@reachyou.com

Objective: area where you make your case. As to what you will do for the employer. Make this section clear and brief. Don't use "I" – as your name is already listed above.

Skill set: Highlight your best skills – example, how many words per minute, problem solving experience, etc.

Education: List in chronological order. List the degree or credential, with the institution, and location. Along with the date of completion on the right side. (When in college, high school is not equal – to the education of a college or university.)

Relevant Coursework: you can add this section – if you've taken courses that related to the job, you're applying for.

Employment: List your past positions (chronologically) with the employer, and their location. On the right hand side – list your starting and ending dates of employment. Then make a list of your work. Everything to highlight what you did. If your employment is impressive/prestigious; you can list this before the education section.

References: List as least three references, make sure you ask – so they are aware – and make sure they are not relatives. Include their profession and contact information; phone number, email, etc.

Example: **Asparagus Green**

223 Cucumber Dr.   (888) 555-9999
Village Leaf, HN 7701   agreen@veggie.com

Objective   To work honestly and
openly; to ensure my
performance of general
manager of operations
reflects well on
Consultants Green Inc.

Skills Set   • 175 words per
minute.
• Bilingual in
Spanish &
French.

Education   *Bachelors of Arts in Greens*   May 2007
Management, Cauliflower
University, Broccoli Village, CP.

Masters of Science in Green Gas   May 2011
Engineering, University of Green
Wealth, Village Leaf, HN.

Employment   *Library Assistant, CU*   August 2005-
Library: May 2007
• *Organized books*
via Dewey
Decimal.
• *Assisted Librarian*
in research.

Example:

Asparagus Green

223 Cucumber Dr.   (888) 555-9999
Village Leaf, HN 7701   agreen@veggie.com

References

Carrot McOrange, Professor – Global Economics, University of Green Wealth, Village Leaf, HN 7211.
(555) 888-9999
Profmcorange@ugw.edu

Cucumber Sally, Librarian – Cauliflower University, Broccoli Village, CP. 8850
(444) 777-8888
sallycu@cu.edu

Lime Bean Penny, Cashier – Green Brew Coffee, Village Leaf, HN 72001.

(555)333-4444
penny@leaf.com

Now that we have gone over a Resume Structure and an Example, the rest of the section contains helpful questions – to help write and re-write your resume as you go along.

Use each page – each time you write a resume, each time you use it to apply.

Resume #_____ Date:_____

❏ Have you used the layout/structure of a resume,
   listed before this questionnaire?

_____

_____

_____

❏ Did you make sure that your highlights of each
   section (education, employment, etc.) presented
   itself loud and clear?

_____

_____

_____

❏ Is your list of references, individuals you know?
   Who will speak good on your behalf?

_____

_____

_____

_____

❏ Are you updating your resume, as you gain higher
   education or experience?

_____

_____

_____

_____

Resume #_____ Date:_____

❑ Have you used the layout/structure of a resume, listed before this questionnaire?

_____

_____

_____

❑ Did you make sure that your highlights of each section (education, employment, etc.) presented itself loud and clear?

_____

_____

_____

❑ Is your list of references, individuals you know? Who will speak good on your behalf?

_____

_____

_____

_____

❑ Are you updating your resume, as you gain higher education or experience?

_____

_____

_____

_____

Resume #_____ Date:_____

❑ Have you used the layout/structure of a resume, listed before this questionnaire?

_____

_____

_____

❑ Did you make sure that your highlights of each section (education, employment, etc.) presented itself loud and clear?

_____

_____

_____

❑ Is your list of references, individuals you know? Who will speak good on your behalf?

_____

_____

_____

_____

❑ Are you updating your resume, as you gain higher education or experience?

_____

_____

_____

_____

Resume #_____ Date:_____

❑ Have you used the layout/structure of a resume, listed before this questionnaire?

_____

_____

_____

❑ Did you make sure that your highlights of each section (education, employment, etc.) presented itself loud and clear?

_____

_____

_____

❑ Is your list of references, individuals you know? Who will speak good on your behalf?

_____

_____

_____

_____

❑ Are you updating your resume, as you gain higher education or experience?

_____

_____

_____

_____

Resume #_____ Date:_____

❑ Have you used the layout/structure of a resume,
listed before this questionnaire?

_____

_____

_____

❑ Did you make sure that your highlights of each
section (education, employment, etc.) presented
itself loud and clear?

_____

_____

_____

❑ Is your list of references, individuals you know?
Who will speak good on your behalf?

_____

_____

_____

_____

❑ Are you updating your resume, as you gain higher
education or experience?

_____

_____

_____

_____

Resume #_____ Date:_____

❏ Have you used the layout/structure of a resume, listed before this questionnaire?

_____

_____

_____

❏ Did you make sure that your highlights of each section (education, employment, etc.) presented itself loud and clear?

_____

_____

_____

❏ Is your list of references, individuals you know? Who will speak good on your behalf?

_____

_____

_____

_____

❏ Are you updating your resume, as you gain higher education or experience?

_____

_____

_____

Cover Letter Structure

This section will consist a format or layout of a cover letter and an example of one. That would ideally go with the resume example, before this section.

This section should help give you a better understanding of a cover letter and how to go about it when writing up a resume – and seeking out a job opening.

The following section contains:
- Cover Letter layout and example.
- Checklist/Critical questions: to check off as you go.
- Note section: to make additional notes.

Use Word, when writing your letter. Convert your letter into a PDF.

Your Name

555 your address   (777)cell number

City, state, zip code   email@reachyou.com

Name of Company   Date

Address of Company

Salutations,

You begin by introducing yourself, and quickly address what position you are applying for. You can elaborate on how interested you are and how you found out about the position. You need to research about the position and company/business. So you can write about how informed you are, about it.

Your second paragraph, will be about you – selling yourself. You can talk about how you love the area; because of your study or previous experience.

Lastly, thank them for reading your letter, and let them know if you will be following up, regarding the position.

Your signature.

Enclosure (letting them know something is accompanying your letter, your resume).

Example:

Asparagus Green

223 Cucumber Dr.   (888) 999-9999

<u>Village Leaf, HN 7701</u>   <u>agreen@veggie.com</u>

Consultants Green Inc.   2/23/12

5567 Sprout Lane

Village Leaf, HN 85856

Dear Ma'am or Sir,

It is a privilege and honor to write to you this day. My name is Asparagus Green and I am very excited to apply for the opening position of General Manger of Operations at Consultants Green Inc. in Village Leaf. I recently found this position on Village Leaf's town job openings subscription email. It is quite clear that the objective at Consultants Green – is to bring clean renewable energy; by consulting with investors and customers interested in holding a stake in this growing industry.

My education ranges in Greens Management and Green Gas Engineering. My interdisciplinary studies – have given me the tools needed to work in this position. I feel this position will harness my potential.

With that, I would like to thank you for reading my letter. Please keep me in mind in your reviewing process. I hope to hear from you, and I will be contacting you in two weeks regarding this position. As I am

Respectfully yours,

Asparagus Green

Asparagus Green, M.S., B.A.

Enclosure

The rest of this section will be a check list with helpful questions to follow.

Just like the resume section, use each page – for every position you apply for. Each time you write up a new cover letter.

Cover Letter # _____ Date:_____

❑ Have you used the layout/structure of a cover letter, listed before this questionnaire?

_____

_____

_____

❑ Did you make use of each paragraph to showcase yourself, and how you would be the perfect fit – for the job?

_____

_____

_____

❑ A cover letter, is meant to show your continued interest in the position, does the letter do that?

_____

_____

_____

_____

❑ Do you feel more confident, having a strong letter – to help your chances?

_____

_____

_____

_____

Cover Letter # _____ Date:_____

❑ Have you used the layout/structure of a cover letter, listed before this questionnaire?

_____

_____

_____

❑ Did you make use of each paragraph to showcase yourself, and how you would be the perfect fit – for the job?

_____

_____

_____

❑ A cover letter, is meant to show your continued interest in the position, does the letter do that?

_____

_____

_____

_____

❑ Do you feel more confident, having a strong letter – to help your chances?

_____

_____

_____

_____

Cover Letter # _____ Date:_____

❑ Have you used the layout/structure of a cover letter, listed before this questionnaire?

_____

_____

_____

❑ Did you make use of each paragraph to showcase yourself, and how you would be the perfect fit – for the job?

_____

_____

_____

❑ A cover letter, is meant to show your continued interest in the position, does the letter do that?

_____

_____

_____

_____

❑ Do you feel more confident, having a strong letter – to help your chances?

_____

_____

_____

_____

Cover Letter # _____ Date:_____

❑ Have you used the layout/structure of a cover
  letter, listed before this questionnaire?

_____

_____

_____

❑ Did you make use of each paragraph to showcase
  yourself, and how you would be the perfect fit –
  for the job?

_____

_____

_____

❑ A cover letter, is meant to show your continued
  interest in the position, does the letter do that?

_____

_____

_____

_____

❑ Do you feel more confident, having a strong letter
  – to help your chances?

_____

_____

_____

_____

Cover Letter # _____ Date:_____

❑ Have you used the layout/structure of a cover letter, listed before this questionnaire?

_____

_____

_____

❑ Did you make use of each paragraph to showcase yourself, and how you would be the perfect fit – for the job?

_____

_____

_____

❑ A cover letter, is meant to show your continued interest in the position, does the letter do that?

_____

_____

_____

_____

❑ Do you feel more confident, having a strong letter – to help your chances?

_____

_____

_____

_____

Cover Letter # _____ Date:_____

❑ Have you used the layout/structure of a cover letter, listed before this questionnaire?

_____

_____

_____

❑ Did you make use of each paragraph to showcase yourself, and how you would be the perfect fit – for the job?

_____

_____

_____

❑ A cover letter, is meant to show your continued interest in the position, does the letter do that?

_____

_____

_____

_____

❑ Do you feel more confident, having a strong letter – to help your chances?

_____

_____

_____

_____

Interview Tips

For this last section – the layout will have tips, you can use during the interviewing process.

First thing to remember, no matter how impressive your resume and cover letter sound to you; what makes it all a winner – is when you receive the call or email for an interview. This can be nerve wrecking; having to go through this process. But, the more practice, the better, you'll get the hang of it.

The following section contains:

- Helpful tips: to consider and have in mind when you go through your interviewing process.
- Note section: to make additional notes.

Interview # _____ Date: _____

➢ After applying, make sure to follow up –
  especially if you've mentioned it your cover letter.

_____

_____

_____

➢ Dress to impress, after setting up an interview
  appointment – go dressed up, first impressions are
  long lasting.

_____

_____

_____

➢ For men, a nice button shirt (preferably white),
  with a nice tie, slacks, dress shoes, would be nice.

_____

_____

_____

_____

➢ For women, a nice button blouse, dress skirt or
  slacks, dress shoes – would be a good choice.

_____

_____

_____

_____

Interview #_____ Date: _____

➢ Before arriving, make sure to do your homework
  – study up the company, leaders, etc.

_____

_____

_____

➢ Know what the company/business is doing, what
  their latest venture is. So you'll be up to speed.
  And you'll be prepared.

_____

_____

_____

➢ Keep good posture – your body language will
  communicate (non-verbally) to the interviewer.

_____

_____

_____

_____

➢ Make good eye-contact, listen and nod to what is
  being said to you. When shaking hands, make sure
  it's web to web.

_____

_____

_____

_____

Interview #_____ Date: _____

➤ Answer the questions honestly and answer with
  an educated response (by doing your homework).

_____

_____

_____

➤ If they ask you, if you have any questions – ask –
  it will show your interest and showoff that you
  know much about them.

_____

_____

_____

➤ When negotiating pay/salary; don't' overbear –
  but, also stand your ground, with civility.

_____

_____

_____

_____

➤ Have confidence, even if you don't get the job;
  you'll learn more for the next round.

_____

_____

_____

_____

Interview #_____ Date: _____

➤ Maintain good time management. Use the time wisely – know that there are other applicants.

_____

_____

_____

➤ Every business, company, firm has different time clocks. Meaning that some may take 6 days or 6 months getting back to you.

_____

_____

_____

➤ Note, that many qualified (including you) may be thrown out. It's just that decision for that "one".

_____

_____

_____

_____

➤ However, some may keep your resume on file; for a while, so there may be some hope.

_____

_____

_____

_____

I had a Professor once say, that going to school, going to class, studying, taking exams, and graduating is the easy part. The hard part, is finding the good job. At first, I didn't understand, now I do.

Don't give up, keep on going and your investments in education, training, etc. will pay off, in due season. Thank you for purchasing this journal, please keep a look out for others. Feel free to leave your review.

Best Wishes,
Daniel A. Garcia

www.ingramcontent.com/pod-product-compliance
Lightning Source LLC
Chambersburg PA
CBHW071203220526
45468CB00003B/1143